IN THE
OCEAN

D0490614

I spy with my little eye...

This edition published in 1999 by
Treehouse Children's Books Ltd.,
West Pennard, Glastonbury, Somerset,
UK BA6 8NN.
Illustrations copyright © 1993 by Steve Cox.
Printed in China.

IN THE
OCEAN

A Flip-the-Flap Book

Richard Powell
Illustrated by Steve Cox

I spy
with
my
little
eye

something beginning with

O

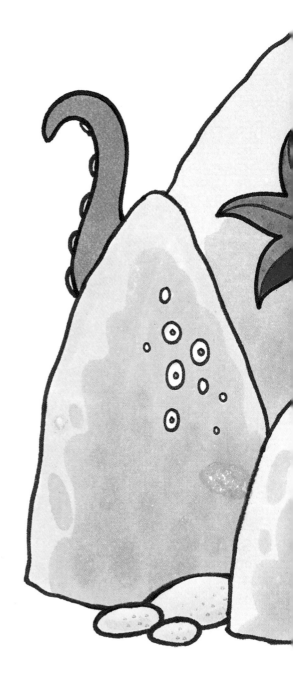

I spy

with

my

little

eye

something beginning with

f

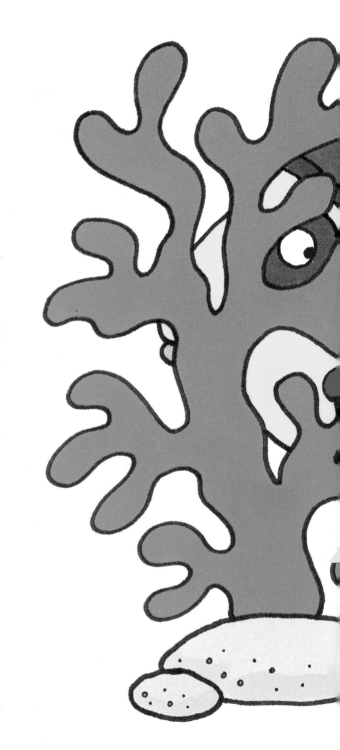

I spy
with
my
little
eye

something beginning with

t

I spy
with
my
little
eye

something beginning with

S

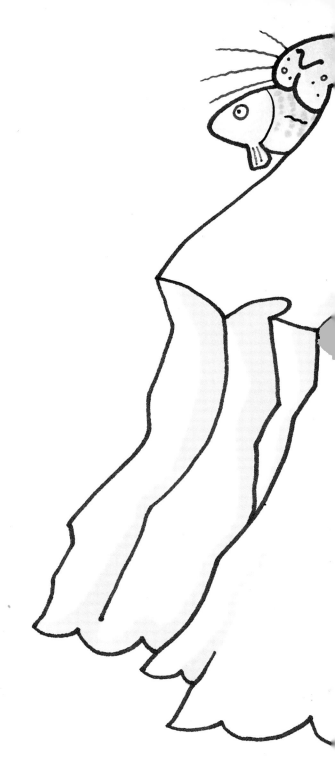

I spy
with
my
little
eye

something beginning with

W

I spy

with

my

little

eye

something beginning with

j

I spy
with
my
little
eye

something beginning with

ee

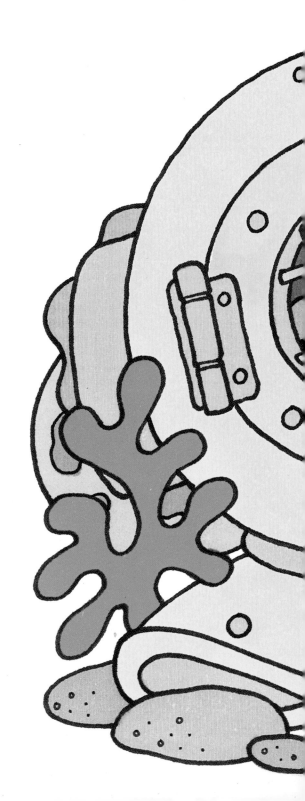

I spy
with
my
little
eye

something beginning with

c

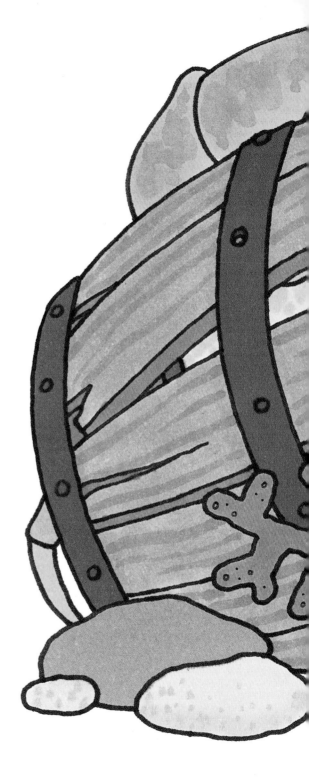

I spy

with

my

little

eye

something beginning with

l

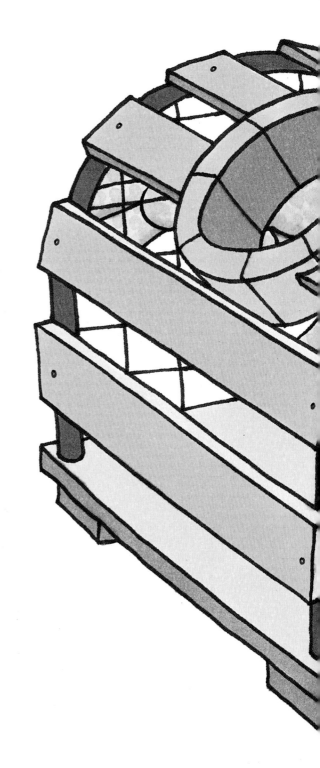

I spy
with
my
little
eye

something beginning with

t

Other Treehouse Flap Books

Wings and Things!	Boyd/Larranaga
Paws to Hug!	Boyd/Larranaga
Ears to Hear!	Boyd/Larranaga
Flippers and Fins!	Boyd/Larranaga
Miaow! Who's in the Garden?	Powell/Cox
Baa! Who's on the Farm?	Powell/Cox
Quack! Who's in the Country?	Powell/Cox
Grrrr! Who's in the Jungle?	Powell/Cox
Woof! Who's at Home?	Powell/Keylock
Nibble! Who's in the Pets' Corner?	Powell/Keylock
If You See a Cow	Powell/Larranaga
If You See a Tiger	Powell/Larranaga
If You See a Mouse	Powell/Larranaga
If You See a Whale	Powell/Larranaga
On The Farm	Powell/Cox
In The Garden	Powell/Cox
In The Jungle	Powell/Cox
In The Ocean	Powell/Cox